HOW "OPEN" SHOULD MY ADOPTION BE?

HOW "OPEN" SHOULD MY ADOPTION BE?

RUSSELL ELKINS

How Open Should My Adoption Be?
Understanding Open vs. Closed Adoption, Preparing for Possible Difficulties, Pros and Cons of Sharing Pictures and Updates, Visiting Birthparents, Social Media, Appropriate Gifts, and More...
part 3 of the series: 30 Minute Guides to Headache-Free Open Adoption Parenting
By Russell Elkins
©2019 Russell Elkins

series line editors: Kim Foster, Jenna Lovell
series content editors: Martin Casey, Cathy Watson Childs

Cover photo and author photo by Jammie Elkins Photography
Cover design by Inky's Nest Design
Interior book layout by Inky's Nest Design

ISBN: 978-1-950741-07-6

Inky's Nest Publishing

RussellElkins.com
2nd edition
First edition printed in 2015 in the United States of America

CONTENTS

Introduction

OPEN & CLOSED ADOPTION

The terms "open adoption" and "closed adoption" used to be very black and white. In decades past, the terms did not even have anything to do with whether or not there was any open communication between biological parents and the child they placed for adoption. The terms simply meant whether or not the birthparents were aware of where the child had been placed.

But that was then.

Nowadays, those two terms mean different things to different people. It is not common anymore for birthparents to be in the dark about where the child was placed. The term "open adoption" evolved to refer to a situation where the adoptive family and biological parents have some form of communication. But even that change came up short because there are so many different levels of communication.

Then came a new term, "semi-open adoption," which referred to adoptions with some form of communication, but that communication is not as open as others. In reality, I would say that this new term is redundant because all open adoptions could be considered semi-open since there one can always find another situation where the adoption is more open than their own in some aspects.

And that is the complexity of open adoption. There are many possible forms of communication between adoptive families and birthparents, especially now that we have social media and the internet to facilitate it. One adoptive family may find it beneficial to have frequent face-to-face visits while another has them rarely or never. One adoptive family may think it best to share pictures once a week while another family chooses to do so once a year. Phone calls. Sharing blogs. Facebook and other social media. Text messaging. The list of ways people can communicate is lengthy.

There is nothing in this world similar to an open adoption relationship. Because of that, it is hard to foresee the many different scenarios that will come. Even though my wife and I did our best to plan ahead, we still found ourselves in the middle of many different situations we had not fully considered.

There comes a time when every hopeful adoptive couple needs to ask themselves the question: *Just how open should our adoption be?* There is no easy answer. Plus, the answer is going to be different for each adoption, even when a couple has adopted more than once. Every adoption relationship is unique.

This book cannot answer that question for you. Only you can do that. What this book will do is give you some serious things to consider in order to help you answer it for yourself.

1

OPEN THE DOOR SLOWLY

Adoptive parents often feel a desire to give the birthparents the world. After all, the birthparents gave them parenthood—one of the greatest gifts a human being could possibly give another, right? With time, however, life settles down. Where does that leave the relationship between the biological parents and adoptive parents? If adoptive parents promise the world, they will not be able to deliver it no matter how badly they want to. On top of that, having a desire to give everything will exhaust the adoptive couple. A person can only endure the feeling of being so deeply in debt for so long before they want to find a way to escape that emotion. If the feeling is so deep that they do not feel like they can ever get out from under it, what choices will they make?

The period of time between when the hopeful adoptive parents are chosen and when placement occurs is intense. My wife and I spent countless hours trying to figure out what we were feeling and deciding what we wanted to do. Once the baby was born, those feelings did not get any easier. They just changed into different things to worry about.

Things do get easier with time, but that first year is usually much more stressful than the following years. Especially during that time, the relationship is still being molded by everybody involved, and everyone needs to adjust.

It is okay for the level of openness to change with time. In fact, I consider that a good thing. It is a good idea to start with things the adoptive couple is sure they can handle and progress from there.

Communication is the key. Even though it is more than okay to say "I don't know" when trying to plan for the future, it is a good idea to try to figure out some sort of structure everyone is comfortable with. If there is no structure, both sides are going to start acting on what they *assume* is the proper level of interaction, and the odds of those two sides being exactly the same are pretty slim. For example, if both sides plan on having face-to-face visits after the birth, but it is not discussed how frequently those interactions will take place, the adoptive couple might think the birthparents will want to come once every three months while the birthparents want to come once every three days. The case is the same with phone calls, letters, pictures, etc.

It is much easier to open a relationship more and more with time than it is to try to work backward. This can be especially tough since the most intense feelings are at the beginning, and the early stages can require the most frequent interaction. If the birthparents are accustomed to a certain level of openness, and the adoptive couple decides they need to close it, it is not easy to do so without risking damage to the relationship. Again, it is much easier to open a relationship more and more with time than it is to work backward. Relationships are not damaged by delivering more than what is expected, especially if both sides feel comfortable with approaching the relationship slowly.

2

SHARING PICTURES

Sharing pictures is a little different than we had expected it to be before our first adoption took place. First of all, there are a million different ways to share pictures. Some people exchange photos through e-mail or regular post. It is common for adoptive parents to let birthparents have access to their Facebook page or family blog. Other people, like my wife and me, have a separate blog set up just for posting pictures and updates about the adopted child and our family.

However the adoptive couple chooses to share pictures, their frame of mind changes with every click of the camera. Adoptive parents have a tendency to want to continually show the birthparents that they made the right decision to choose them, and every photo is a window into the adoptive home. We try a little extra hard to look our best in those pictures. Not only that, but pictures are usually expected on some sort of regularity with open adoptions. No matter if pictures are shared once a day or once a decade, it is not the same as sharing pictures with my other family members.

At first, it felt like we were being monitored. The birthparents were not doing anything out of the ordinary to make us feel this way, but just the act of sending them pictures made us feel like we were had to answer to somebody else—as if someone else were above us on the totem pole. Nobody likes to feel that way, but as time went on and the birthparents showed us that they supported and sustained us as the parents, sharing pictures not only became easier, but also became something enjoyable.

How Often Should I Share Photos?

It is hard to know exactly how often to share them. Some open adoptions have that decision made prior to finalizing. With a lot of adoptions, like ours, the frequency has changed. In the beginning we posted pictures a lot, and as time went by that frequency decreased. That was by design, and was something we discussed early on with the birthparents. We knew they would have a greater need for pictures during the earlier stages after placement, so we were willing to help out with that need. We enjoy sharing photos now, even though it can be time consuming.

What Kinds of Pictures Should I Share?

Be sure to include all kinds of pictures. Although you will be tempted to try to look your best in each snapshot, do not worry so much about that. Let them see you with your hair down. Show your casual side. Be natural.

Above all, let them see you loving this child. It may be uncomfortable at times for them to look upon you snuggling the child they are not able to raise, but that is why they chose you. They want to see that this child is loved in the way they know this child deserves.

3

FACEBOOK & OTHER SOCIAL MEDIA

When my wife and I were adopting for the first time, our son's birthmother, Brianna, first contacted us via email. She got our email address from the adoption agency. We exchanged a small handful of emails throughout that first day, and although we were incredibly nervous, we were also very excited. That same evening my wife and I both discovered that she was requesting to connect with us on Facebook. We pondered it for a moment, then accepted her request. Like many people, we did not know at the time that Facebook would catapult our adoption into the "wide open" realm of open adoption.

We spent two hours in a Facebook chat with Brianna that first night. Both sides were very excited to get to know each other and chatting online proved to be a relaxed way of doing just that. A candid chat was more intimate than our emails had been. We called each other by telephone periodically, but many times during those phone conversations we found ourselves in awkward silence. Awkward silence magnified itself tenfold over the phone because of the intensity and inherent awkwardness of the situation. I can carry on an hour long conversation with my brother on the phone and enjoy every second of it, but trying to make small talk with a fifteen-year-old girl was very different. My wife did have an easier time on the phone with her than I did, largely because girls are just better at that sort of thing, but Facebook chat was a lot easier. Facebook played a big role in helping us bond with Brianna from the very beginning.

Are You Ready to Give Up Your Privacy?

In addition to spending so much time chatting with her live, we were able to follow her on a daily basis. She did the same with us. That was both a blessing and a curse. It was a blessing because we were able to enjoy the interaction and we were able to see her in her own element. The curse was that by connecting this way, both sides gave up a lot of our right to privacy.

One of the most difficult things about Facebook is that once you have connected with someone it is difficult to disconnect without hurting the relationship. Adoptive parents and birthparents tend to become intimately interested in one another, to the point where they nearly stalk one another. Facebook will not send the birthparents a notice if the adoptive parents "unfriend" them, but if they are used to following updates on a regular basis and then suddenly do not have access to them anymore, they are going to notice. And if that was done without discussing it first, it is likely that will hurt their feelings. Even if other parts of the adoption remain just as open as they have always been, there is always potential of hurt feelings when one part of it closes, especially if they have been following you closely.

Also, adoption has a tendency to take over the minds of adoptive parents to the point where they have a difficult time thinking about anything else. It can be exhausting to focus on the same thing all day, day in and day out. If you are on Facebook a lot and you are friends with your child's birth-parents, there is a good chance you will obsess about their Facebook page too.

Is it Possible to Control What Is Posted on Your Social Media Page?

Jammie and I found that our Facebook experience changed over time. We were first contacted by Brianna halfway through her pregnancy so we had quite a few months to get to know each other. We enjoyed our interaction, but we found that we had to watch our words very carefully once time came close to our son being born. We wanted to share many things with the rest of our friends regarding our upcoming adoption, but many times we refrained from doing so because we knew Brianna would be following our posts. Placing a child for adoption was likely to be one of the most heart-wrenching and difficult things Brianna would ever go through, so we did not feel comfortable celebrating with all of our Facebook friends right there in front of her. We did not want our page to be full of congratulations for her to read.

You cannot control what other people say. Most people in the world do not fully understand open adoption, so some of your friends may post really ignorant things on your page. It is bound to happen. While it is true that you have the ability to delete your friends' comments, it is only a matter of time before your child's birthparents see one before you do. And how are they going to feel when you know your child's birthparents read a post from your aunt that says, "That is so neat that you were able to save that baby from the life he would have had with that unstable girl," or even something as simple as, "That baby is so lucky to have you!" The situation is already delicate, and adding your friends into the mix via Facebook adds a level of communication that is difficult for you to control.

Are You Comfortable with the Birthparents Sharing Photos of Your Child?

You also need to discuss whether or not you are comfortable with your child's birthparents sharing photos of the child on their own Facebook page. Some people are comfortable with this, some are not. When considering this, keep in mind that your child's birthparents are thinking constantly about the adoption—especially during that first year. They need to heal. Even if they feel they did the right thing they will need to come to terms with the loss they just experienced by placing that child into your arms. Allowing them to share your pictures online can help them in this healing process. As much as you wish you could just take away the pain they are feeling, they need their own support group, which usually means their close family and friends. Facebook can be a good tool for birthparents to share their intimate world with that support group.

If you do decide to allow them to share your pictures, you must keep in mind that their friends and family are not connected to you like the birthparents are. When they see pictures of that baby, they will see the child through the lens of their connection to the birthparents. They will usually talk about it being the child of the birthparents, often times as if you do not even exist. How will you feel when someone says, "Oh Callie, your baby is so adorable!" Or even something as simple as, "Do you think he'll grow up to be as tall as his daddy?"

Will it hurt your feelings if the birthmom only shares pictures of the baby and never includes any of the pictures that include you in them? Or better yet, since cropping photos is common on Facebook, how will you feel if the photo is cropped to include just the child, and you have been cropped out? That might seem harsh, but it is common.

What Risks Come with Accepting a Friend Request from the Birthparents' Friends?

If you decide to be Facebook friends with the birthparents' friends, you are opening up a whole new level of the relationship over which you have no control.

Jammie and I started out on Facebook by allowing Brianna's close friends to connect with us. That came with some serious problems, though. We did have a beautiful relationship with Brianna, but we did not have a good relationship with Daren, our son's birthfather. We tried to reach out to him on numerous occasions, offering to share updates and pictures with him, but each time he declined. Since some of Brianna's friends were also Daren's friends, things got complicated. At the same time we were offering to send Daren photos and he was refusing them, one of Brianna's friends, whom we had connected with on Facebook, was downloading and sending him the photos. That may not sound like a big deal since we were already trying to offer him pictures, but it clearly showed us that there were layers to our open adoption that were out of our control. That made us very uncomfortable, so we made the decision to sever ties with the fringes of our adoption circle, and unfriended everyone on Facebook except for Brianna and her immediate family. We also asked Brianna not to post any pictures of our son for a while and she was onboard with that decision.

Is it a Good Idea to Follow an Adoption-Related Facebook Page?

Another dynamic to the Facebook world are the many different public pages out there. My wife and I used to manage an adoption page that had a large global following. That page served as a public forum where people from all over the world could come to share experiences, ask questions, celebrate adoption, and seek support through difficult times.

It is important for people to keep in mind that, although my wife and I are located in Idaho and someone responding to our post might live in England, there is still a good possibility that whatever I type on a public forum will get back to my child's biological parents. It is more common than you might think. It may seem unlikely that you will both stumble on the same page and read one another's comment, but the more popular a page is the more likely it you will both end up there. If not that, it is quite possible that one of your birth-parents friends could stumble upon it and tell them about the comment you made. Since adoption is at the forefront of both of your minds, it is not uncommon for both sides to go looking for public adoption pages where you might find likeminded people.

I encourage you to join one of these online communities, whether on Facebook or somewhere else. They are a great way to educate yourself about adoption situations and seek comradery with those in similar situations to yours. But I must warn you: *Never share something publically that you would not want your child's birthparents to read.*

How Well Does Facebook Serve for Sharing Photos with the Birthparents?

Facebook is a great place to share pictures without effort. As discussed before, sharing pictures can become difficult and time consuming. With the invention of the smart phone and other devices, many people have a camera on them at all times. It is easy to snap a picture when your kid is in the middle of doing something funny, and to put it on Instagram and Facebook. This is a great way to take the load off of your shoulders. It keeps the pictures candid, frequent, and spontaneous.

While it is a great way to be spontaneous and candid, I do not recommend this to be your *only* form of sharing pictures. Facebook and Instagram downsize every picture you upload. This means that the quality is significantly reduced, which also means that if a birthparent ever wants to print a photo to place on their desk at work, the quality is going to turn out terrible. If you choose to share pictures on social media platforms, you should consider sharing somewhere else as well. I recommend also sending pictures via email, traditional post, or uploading them to a blog where the quality will not be compromised.

Did You Know You Can Have More Than One Facebook Account?

You can change your security settings on Facebook, and I highly recommend doing so. If you know how to work Facebook properly, you can choose with every post who can and who cannot see your post.

Some people create a whole separate page just for the birthparents to follow. This could be the solution for many people who do not want to involve a bunch of extra people, or for those who want to share with the birthparents but do not want to give away their privacy on their regular page. It is not difficult to do.

If I Could Go Back, Would I Connect Again on Facebook?

As I mentioned before, we connected on Facebook with Brianna on the very same day we had been contacted. There were times when we felt uncomfortable with the connection, but if I could go back and talk to my former self about everything I have learned in hindsight, I do not think I would change a thing. Facebook made it possible for us to really connect. It was a big part of getting to know each other, especially since there were so many miles between us.

Our second adoption was a different story. We adopted a baby girl from someone who lived only a short drive away. We got to know each other face-to-face, sometimes meeting at the adoption agency and sometimes in our own home. Because of this intimate connection, we did not feel Facebook was necessary for us. We really enjoyed celebrating our adoption with all of our family and friends on Facebook, something we did not get to do when Brianna was following our posts the first time. About six months after that adoption was final, after the initial intense emotions of the adoption simmered, we then connected on Facebook with our daughter's birthparents.

Connecting from the beginning was the right thing to do for our first adoption. Waiting until six months after for our second adoption was the right thing to do with that one. Everything depends on the situation.

4

BLOGS & EMAIL

My wife set up a blog just for Brianna. That was the primary method we used for a long time to share updates and pictures. We made the blog password-protected and gave Brianna permission to share that password with whomever she wanted.

There have always been a number of people interested in our adoption besides those in our immediate adoption triad. Brianna shared the password with her parents and her siblings as well as a few close friends. This made it possible for Brianna to share that part of her life with those important to her—those she needed to lean on for love and support.

Perhaps the most beneficial thing about using a blog to share updates was that our children's birthparents could check it whenever they wanted. Each one the birthparents have gone through times when they felt so overwhelmed by adoption

RUSSELL ELKINS

that they needed a break. A blog makes it possible to do that. Facebook is so "in your face" that it will not give someone time away. It is difficult for birthparents to resist opening a letter on the day it arrives, whether it be email or traditional post. Blogs are always there, though, and the birthparents can choose when to visit the page and when to avoid it. They can go weeks or months without reading updates, then when they feel ready to visit the page, they can catch up on all the time spent away. On the days when they feel especially nostalgic, they can go back through and read again all the posts from the past, even ones from long ago.

What Are the Pros and Cons of Using a Blog for Sharing Photos?

One benefit of using a blog is that it provides the ability to load pictures at full quality. Birthparents parents can print them out and admire them when they are not connected to an internet device.

Blogs make it easy to load multiple pictures all at once.

The obvious con about sharing photos via the use of a blog is that it does take more effort to load pictures compared to using email or social media. This is nothing that would overwhelm an adoptive couple who have an agreement to share pictures just once every six months or so, but for those who plan to share with more regularity it could.

Did You Know a Blog Can Serve as a Journal for You?

Another benefit to a blog that we did not anticipate is that it also serves as a journal. After a significant amount of time had passed, my wife and I realized how much fun it was *for ourselves* to look back at all the many things we had gone through and shared on the site. There are many online companies that can take your blog posts and print them up for you in the form of a book—a priceless keepsake.

Should You Keep More than One Blog?

You have to ask yourself how many blogs you want to update. Some adoptive parents simply allow the biological parents access to the family blog they already keep. This makes it so that they do not have to update more than one, and this works out very well for them.

Others do not like this idea because they want to talk about things that might be sensitive to their adoption situation. For example, some people are not comfortable complaining about the difficulties of parenthood (late nights, feeling inadequate, etc.) knowing that the birthparents are on the other end hearing them whine.

31

When we adopted the first time, my wife created a separate blog just for Brianna.

When we adopted for a second time, she created two new blogs—one for the new birthmother, and the other for the new birthfather. We visited face-to-face frequently with the birthparents at that time and we usually took pictures when we were together. We wanted to share those pictures on our blogs, but we were uncomfortable sharing them with everybody. We wanted to save Darci (birthmother) from having to stare at pictures of her ex-husband while trying to enjoy pictures of baby Hazel. So my wife, Jammie, was busy keeping our own personal family blog updated as well as three more blogs for the birth families. This was never something we planned to do forever—just for the first little while when everyone's emotions were still at their peak intensity.

Then the inevitable happened. We accidentally posted pictures of Darci's ex-husband on her blog from a time we went to visit with his family. She did not like that much at all. On top of the fact that maintaining so many blogs created a lot of extra work for us, that incident helped us see just how complicated we had made the process of sharing photos. It was too much. From that point on we combined all three adoption blogs into one and only posted things that were okay to share with all of them. If we had a picture or update that we wanted to share with only one person, we did that through email.

5

FACE-TO-FACE VISITS

Having an open adoption with emails, blog posts, and Facebook chats is one thing. Being able to see each other face-to-face is quite different. It can bring your adoption up to a whole new level of intimacy and "openness."

We got to know Brianna really well before our son was born. We did not only get to know her through social media, but we got to know her face-to-face. She wanted to come to Idaho to have her baby, and since she did not want travel during the last two months of her pregnancy, she came early. And can you guess where she stayed during those two months? That's right. Although we had a place lined up for her to stay, we became so comfortable together that she just stayed with us in our guest room. You can read the whole story in my book *Open Adoption, Open Heart: An Adoptive Father's Inspiring Journey.*

We saw her every day for ten weeks straight before she headed back to her hometown two thousand miles away. Although we were in regular contact after she went back home, when she called us up to tell us that she was planning to come visit, we were terrified. We did not know what to expect. Would her presence make us feel like we were somehow less important? Would she try to play the motherly role, diminishing everything Jammie had done over the last year? Would her visit somehow erase all the progress we had made over the last year in our relationship with her? There were a thousand things we worried about, and there was no way to answer them until she showed up.

She came with her older sister this time, whom we had never met before. Even though Brianna was only sixteen at the time, she had a great head on her shoulders and went out of her way to calm our worries. It did not take long before we were able to remember just how much we loved having her around. She was a blessing in our home, not a hindrance.

The visit was not easy. Even though the visit was amazing and increased the love we have for one another, a person can only handle so much emotional stimuli before reaching overload. It is possible to have too much of a good thing, and a long face-to-face visit is emotionally very intense. There came a point when Brianna wanted to pull back and have some time alone, but that was difficult since she was staying in our home. Jammie and Brianna spent a few hours having a heart-to-heart talk, and they were able to work through it together. They are awesome that way.

Brianna came again a year later, and even though we were now two years removed from the adoption, it still was not much easier. Our son had become a lot more interactive since she had last seen him. That brought the intensity of the visit up yet another notch, and Jammie and Brianna spent a lot of time talking working through the difficulties together. Things were similar the third time she came to visit.

Our second adoption was even more intense. Our daughter's birthmother, Darci, lived in the area. Caleb, the birthfather, lived a few hours away. Because of this, we were introduced to a whole new level of interaction we had not learned to deal with during our first adoption. While Darci did not spend the night at our house like Brianna did, she would ask for permission to come visit frequently. Sometimes she would call a day in advance and other times right before coming.

For us, a three day visit from Brianna was actually less stressful than three short visits within a month from Darci. Since she visited so often, and since we did not usually plan very far ahead for those visits, we found ourselves always feeling the intensity of the situation. Adoption is intense, and so much spontaneity made it so that our visits were never far from our mind. We woke up each day not knowing if she was going to come visit, so we spent each day in the intense emotions that accompanied a visit. We felt this intensity of emotion even on the days Darci did not come. It wore us out.

We spent six months like that—some months with many visits, and some months with none. We decided it was time for some structure. We were still happy to have Darci in our home, but we discussed creating some sort of schedule. This was awkward to do since creating structure around something where Darci was used having none felt like we were closing a part of the adoption, but she soon understood our need to do so. We gave her the freedom of choosing the frequency of those visits. What we mostly needed was to be able to plan ahead, to ready ourselves emotionally, and to be able to relax between visits. If you are interested in reading that full story, part two of the series is called *Open Adoption, Open Arms.*

The intensity of the situation does not last forever. It diminishes with time. Although the visits still had their difficulties, Brianna's second visit was a little bit easier than the first, and her third visit was easier than the second.

Darci's visits grew more relaxed every time as well. At the time of this publication (second edition), it has been eight years since our second adoption took place. Our relationship with Darci has taken different forms, from multiple visits in the same week to going a few years without any contact at all.

We still have structure around our visits with Darci. In fact, we still have structure around our visits with all of our children's birthparents. Caleb, the birthfather from our second adoption, is the birthparent we see most frequently, but we have been through so much over these eight years together that the structure helps us keep our relationship healthy.

Although the only role he played in our first adoption was that of periodically popping into Brianna's life to harass her, we have even connected with our son's birthfather. Some of our relationships have remained healthy the entire time while some of our other relationships have not. Our relationships have changed dramatically over time as our children's birthparents have graduated from college, begun their careers, gotten married and even had children of their own. You can read about all of our ups and downs with these relationships over the years with our children's birthparents in part three of the series entitled *Open Adoption, Open Mind.*

Do You Want Family Members to Have Close Relationships with Birthparents?

Just like with social media, when you mix other people into the picture, things get more complicated. This is even *more* evident with face-to-face visits than it is Facebook or any other form of contact.

It is important to understand that people outside your tight adoption triad (adoptive parents, birthparents, and the child) do not understand your situation as well as they think they do. People say horribly insensitive or ignorant things at times, and when that happens while you are in the presence of the birthparents, how are you going to feel?

You need to decide whether or not your own family members are going to have a relationship with your child's biological family. Many people have told me that, because the birthparents already feel like family, it only feels natural to have them interact with the rest of their family. Jammie and I do not feel the same way.

The way Jammie and I see it, open adoption is so complicated already that we do not need extra layers of complexity. And by "extra layers" I mean extra people, even the people we love the most. My family is awesome. Jammie's family is awesome. Brianna's family is awesome. But there really is no need for my sister to have a close relationship with Brianna.

We wanted to keep our complicated situation as simple as possible, but that was not the only reason we chose to keep those connections separate. We also wanted our close friends and family to think of us first when they are around our kids. When my Mom is playing with her grandson, I do not want her to think of him any differently than she would think of my brother's son. It has nothing to do with my insecurities or selfishness, I just think my son deserves to have his extended family look at him the same as they would anyone else in the family. If my sister were to have a close and loving relationship with Darci, would she think of Darci first when holding our daughter?

As the years have gone by, we have found ourselves in numerous instances when family has mingled with our children's biological families and no problems have arisen from those visits. Still, it is nice to keep some complicated situations simple.

Do You Want to Have a Relationship with Others from the Birthparents' Family?

While my parents do not have a relationship with Brianna, Darci or Caleb, it is not the same the other way around. Jammie and I do have a relationship with our children's biological grandparents and it is wonderful! Our daughter, Hazel, was their first biological grandchild on Caleb's side and I shudder at the thought of keeping that away from them. They love her so much and we love having them part of our family.

It is important to keep in mind that the further you get away from your inner circle, the less likely someone is to know how to properly act around your adoption. You may have stopped using inappropriate terms like "giving up a child" or "the real father," but your child's biological aunt or uncle will probably still say those types of things.

When considering this level of openness, you must also understand one very important fact: many people on the biological side may not see you as the parents. I do not mean to say that they will belittle you on purpose or talk to you like you have kidnapped the child, but there is a good chance they will see things differently than your family does.

In a common adoption scenario, the biological grandma would have been present through the whole pregnancy watching the expecting mother's belly grow and anticipating the baby's arrival. When that child was born, she had either barely met you or she did not know you at all. Even if she is completely onboard with the idea of adoption, in her eyes that baby is the offspring of her own family tree. It is natural for her to see it that way. Even if she acknowledges and loves you for your role in the child's life, there is a strong possibility that she will always connect that child to her own bloodline first, not through you.

And again, the further you get away from your intimate inner circle, the more likely it is that someone will say something that can hurt your feelings. Every family has a member who talks before thinking, so if your level of openness means that you find yourself at a biological family gathering, plan on crazy Uncle Joe cornering you to make you feel like you are just babysitting his niece's kid. If that does not happen, awesome. At least you were prepared for it.

Who Should Be Holding the Child When You Are All Together?

Who gets to hold your child? That question might sound less important, but you will want to discuss it before the child is born. Everyone feels differently about it, so you will want to know where the birthparents stand.

Jammie and I had to consider the feelings of the birthparents. Some birthparents, like Brianna, enjoy holding the child as much as possible. Others, like Darci, feel uncomfortable holding the child too much. The trauma associated with the adoption sometimes came flooding back to her mind when she held baby Hazel, so Jammie and I did our best to stay in tune with what she was feeling.

We told Brianna, Darci and Caleb that we would not place a child into their arms without them asking for it. They know they can ask to hold the child whenever then desire and they do just that. That system works well for us and we do not have to worry about whether or not we are forcing something on them. Of course, our system would not work if the birthparents were timid or felt uncomfortable asking to hold the child.

Also keep in mind that some birthparents can be overbearing. If Brianna wanted to hold our son the whole time we were together without letting us do so, that would certainly make us feel uncomfortable. It would make us feel like we were unimportant while Brianna was around—like we were just babysitters for her kid. If we had a birthparent who behaved like that, our current system would not work.

The decision is not only up to the birthparents. We are a team. Jammie and I have needs just like the birthparents do, and those matter just as much as the needs of the birthparents. Because of this, we discuss all of these topics regularly.

Do You Want Visits to Take Place in Your Own Home?

Having visits in your own home has its ups and downs. Just the thought of having an open door to your adoption can add another layer of stress. There is something inherently intimate about allowing someone into your own home—your castle. That is the most intimate location in your life, and opening that up to someone means that you are opening up an intimate part of yourself to them. Especially in the earlier days, whenever a birthparent came over for a visit we scrubbed every inch of the house, even if it was already clean. We wanted them to see how awesome we are—how marvelous of a choice they made by choosing us to parent their child. During those first few visits we felt more anxiety about our home than we did when the caseworkers came over to inspect our house for the required homestudy.

That said, there is also something wonderful and intimate about sharing that part of us. When we visit in our own home, we do not have to worry about wind ruining our picnic at the park. We do not have to worry about a waiter hinting that we have been taking up space in their restaurant for too long (both of those things have happened to us). I love the time we spend together in our home and would not trade it for the world, but I can also see clearly why some people prefer to do all of their visits in public places.

Is it Okay to Experience Major Life Events Away from the Birthparents?

With open adoption, we share so much of our lives that there comes a point where we all need to be allowed to have something just for ourselves. Everybody has to draw a line somewhere and say, "No, this is mine. This is not for sharing." Since open adoption tends to magnify every emotion, it is that much more important to decide which things you just do not want to share.

Some of those things might be special events. Even if you have a wide open adoption, does that mean you need to invite the birthparents to everything? Is it okay not to invite the birthparents to your child's christening or baptism? The child's first birthday party?

It is okay to keep some things just for yourself. It is all right to want to feel "normal" once in a while by just doing something on your own. There is nothing wrong with that. Keep some things for yourselves. If you do not, you run the risk of feeling like someone else is controlling your life. Just what those things are will depend on what you need. They will be different for every adoptive couple.

Is it Okay for Birthparents to Play the Role of Babysitter?

My wife and I have counseled with a lot of adoptive parents over the years and we have seen this become a hot topic for a lot of people. Just last week my wife and I were talking with an adoptive mother friend who has become overwhelmed with the way their child's birthmother has become overbearing with telling them things they should and should not do as parents. This birthmother still wants to play the role of mother, but that role is no longer hers to play. And since they have been allowing her to play the role of temporary caretaker, they have painted themselves into a corner where it is difficult to take that away without damaging their relationship.

My wife and I have never allowed our children's birthparents to babysit our children, but our reasons are not because we think they would try to tell us how we needed to parent. Especially during the times when our children were babies, we know that allowing them to babysit would have been overwhelming for all people involved, but even more so for the birthparents. Adoption is complicated enough without putting ourselves in scenarios that would play with people's emotions.

I do have some close friends who allow babysitting and it works well for them. They allow the birthparents to babysit on occasion as well as the birth grandparents to do so. These members of the birthparents family have always treated their situation with care and consider it a great honor to be allowed to play that role. I am not aware of anything ever happening during their babysitting time that has hurt the relationship between birthparents and adoptive parents.

Having seen instances of babysitting working out well and babysitting turning out to be a complete disaster, I recommend adoptive parents tread very carefully through this matter. Adoptive parents should give this topic a bit more consideration than usual before moving forward with something like this.

How Much is Open Adoption Like Co-Parenting?

Before the adoption takes place, all of the parenting decisions are on the shoulders of the expecting parents, not on those of the hopeful adoptive couple. Once the adoption has become final, those roles switch.

Open adoption is not co-parenting. Allow me to repeat that for emphasis—open adoption is not co-parenting. Birthparents do not have any more say in parenting decisions than would, say, the next door neighbor or the stranger across town. Some people find that concept hard to grasp because that child grew in the belly of the birthmother, not in the adoptive mother. Some people find that concept hard to grasp because the birthparents love this child with all their heart and the only thing they want is the best for the child. Some people find that concept hard to grasp because they feel like the adoptive couple is in debt for the wonderful gift they have been given of parenthood. But that is not how adoption works.

Adoptive parents who allow people outside their home to dictate (or even have a say) in the decisions for their home are doing their child a disservice. Every child should be entitled to a strong foundation at home where the decision-making process is not fluid. There needs to be no question about who has the authority to make decisions and who holds the trump card. This means that if the adoptive parents and birthparents disagree on something major like whether or not to vaccinate, public school vs. home school or private school, whether or not the adoptive parents should take a new job and move far away, that those decisions are to be made by the adoptive parents according to what they deem important for their home. This also means that the small decisions like haircuts and where to hold birthday parties are not to be made by the birthparents.

Open adoption is not similar to the scenario of divorced parents where two households have a say in decisions. Open adoption is not co-parenting.

6

GIFTS

Is It Okay for the Children to Receive Gifts After the Adoption Takes Place?

There is no rule about who gives presents and when they should be given, nor should there be. Jammie and I have made the decision that anybody can give gifts at any time, but they will never be asked to. And yes, that means that some people in our adoption circle give presents often, and others never do.

It just so happens that the people who share gifts with us always send one for both of our kids, not just the one they are related to biologically. It is nice to know that they care enough about our family to take that into account. That is the type of relationship we have built. Although there is naturally a tighter connection to the child from their own bloodline, they love all of us dearly.

47

We did not want the birthparents in our lives to feel obligated to send presents, so we told them that right up front. They do not need to unless they feel inclined. Sometimes they do, sometimes they do not. That is fine with us.

You should also keep in mind that if you allow the birthparents (and their families) to give gifts however they choose, that they will each choose differently. As is the case with our family where we have more than once adopted child, the birthparents of one of our two children give gifts a lot more often than the birthparents of the other child. I expect that this would be quite common for situations like ours. So you would need to discuss without your children and ask yourselves how you will feel if you allow one set of birthparents to spoil your kids more than the other birthparents. Again, our childrens' birthparents give gifts to both children when they do give presents, so potential issues of jealousy have been kept at bay, but it is easy to see how an unbalance in gift-giving could be problematic with the children.

What About Giving Gifts to the Potential Birthparents Before the Adoption Takes Place?

Keep in mind that what I have said about presents does not include giving gifts around or before the time of placement. If you are thinking about giving someone a gift during that time, be absolutely sure you know and understand the laws within your state. In many states it is illegal to give a gift before the adoption is completely finalized in the courts. This is because presents can be seen as a form of coercion. In other words, you do not want to ever be seen as someone who is trying to pressure an expecting parent into choosing adoption, or choosing you. You can find yourself in a lot of legal trouble if you give gifts or money in a state where it is not allowed.

7

IN THE HOSPITAL
DELIVERY ROOM

Jammie and I were lucky enough to be invited to the delivery room during the birth of both of our children. That invitation was something that we will always be able to cherish. That was a very sacred time for us.

It is very important for hopeful adoptive parents to understand one basic point with regards to the hospital: The time at the hospital belongs to the biological parents, not the hopeful adoptive parents. If you keep that in your mind at all times, you will be fine.

That means that, first of all, you do not invite yourself to the hospital or even ask the expecting mother if you can come. You wait for an invitation, and only if you are extended that invitation do you show up.

Brianna and Darci's mothers were both present during delivery. While Jammie and I did our best to help out, it was not our role to be the primary supporter. We ran errands when we were asked and gave support where we could, but we never jumped in to try to be a bigger part of the situation than we deserved to be.

We were guests to *their* big day. That meant that we were not in a position to invite any of our friends to come to the hospital, and trust me when I say that we had a lot of friends and family who wanted to come by and see us.

We were in the hospital for more than two days when Brianna gave birth, and after a while the intensity of the situation simmered down enough that we felt comfortable allowing my mother, my brother and his wife, and Jammie's best friend to stop by. They stayed for a very short while and that was it.

At the hospital for our second adoption, we were also there for two days but the situation was so delicate that we never allowed any of our family or friends to join us. We even had friends show up unannounced to the hospital with hopes of visiting with us but we turned them away.

With both hospital visits, Jammie and I were quick to excuse ourselves from the room if we felt Brianna, Darci or Caleb needed time alone with the baby. Those moments at the hospital were very intense, perhaps the most intense times of the whole process. Every time we watched Brianna, Darci or Caleb hold their baby, we wondered if they would be able to go through with the adoption. At the same time that we longed so badly to become parents, we knew that we should not pressure them in any way. We made it our goal to be there to assist, and to never look at the hospital time as our chance to start assuming the role of "parent." There would be plenty of time for that after the child came home with us.

Conclusion

Every open adoption is unique. Jammie and I have adopted twice, but the two situations are very different from each other. You cannot look upon someone else's adoption, even if it is a wonderful situation that you would like to emulate, and expect your situation to be just like theirs. That does not mean your situation is somehow better or worse—it is just different.

Only you know what is right for your home. As soon as you announce to the world that you are hoping to adopt, and especially after that child comes into your home, people will bombard you with opinions and information. Some of those opinions will come from people have been in similar situations, but much of it will come from people who only think they know what they are talking about. Take it all for what it is worth. You should not write someone off just because they have never been in your shoes, but you should also not accept their advice just because they have a strong opinion. Whether other people think that your adoption is too open, or too closed, it does not matter. You are the decision makers. You are the parents.

You owe it to yourself, your child, and the biological parents to plan as much as you can before the adoption takes place. Many states and adoption agencies require the hopeful adoptive couple and biological parents to have a formal discussion about the different aspects of an adoption relationship. If your situation does not require this, I strongly suggest you still make it a priority. The less you communicate, the more you are assuming and hoping the other side feels the same way you do. And the more you are assuming, the more you are gambling with the relationship.

There are many things you cannot fully anticipate until you are completely immersed in the situation, but you must not use that as an excuse. Learn as much as you can before you adopt. This book is part of the *Guide to a Headache-Free Adoption* series. I have also released three books that tell all of the intimate details of our adoption story entitled *Glass Half-Full Adoption Memoirs*. My goal in writing that series was to bring you as close as possible to feeling like you actually lived through the experience with us. You will read about the good times and the difficult. You will see some of the difficult decisions we made and why we made them. Most importantly, you will be able to ask yourself what *you* would do if you were in our shoes.

Open adoption relationships are not easy. Those who have "ideal" situations have reached that point because both sides have worked hard at it. Communicate with one another *before and after* placement. Base your relationship on realistic expectations of one another, not on what you think someone wants you to say or do. Above all, love each other despite everyone's imperfections. We all have them, and they can seem especially apparent while you are in such an intense emotional situation. That same intensity can also bond you together in a relationship truly unique in this world.